INNOCENT SCREAMS

David Pownall

INNOCENT SCREAMS

OBERON BOOKS
LONDON

First published in 2009 by Oberon Books Ltd
Electronic edition published in 2013

Oberon Books Ltd
521 Caledonian Road, London N7 9RH
Tel: +44 (0) 20 7607 3637 / Fax: +44 (0) 20 7607 3629
e-mail: info@oberonbooks.com
www.oberonbooks.com

A catalogue record for this book is available from the British
Library.

PB ISBN: 978-1-84002-611-5
E ISBN: 978-1-78319-405-6

eBook conversion by Replika Press PVT Ltd, India.

Visit www.oberonbooks.com to read more about all our books
and to buy them. You will also find features, author interviews and
news of any author events, and you can sign up for e-newsletters
so that you're always first to hear about our new releases.

Characters

BACON

PAREJA

INNOCENT

VELAZQUEZ

FLAMINIA

OLYMPIA

Act One

June 1953. The middle of the night. FRANCIS BACON's chaotic and messy studio in Reece Mews, London SW7. A gold and velvet throne stands centre. The sound of a car drawing up outside. Slam of car door. The car drives away. Pause. Noisy climbing of stairs. A stumble, shout and fall. Nervous laughter. A key rattles in a lock. An offstage door opens noisily, then closes. The light in the studio is turned on. BACON enters, dressed in a black leather jacket and holding a bloody handkerchief to his mouth. He is supported by PAREJA, the mulatto slave of Velazquez.

PAREJA: Let me have a look at your face in the light. (*He gently examines an injury to BACON's mouth.*) Does it hurt?

BACON shakes his head.

Why did he do this to you?

BACON: Because I asked him to.

PAREJA: You're crazy.

BACON: Really?

PAREJA: Are you looking for death?

BACON: Bring me Mr Pamphili.

PAREJA: Why do you need him yet again?

BACON: Do as you're told!

PAREJA: Why is this picture taking such an age?

BACON: That's my business.

PAREJA: That's what you said last time, and the time before that, and the time before that. Isn't doing this picture costing you money?

BACON: Tonight is my last try. I'm going to pull out all the stops.

PAREJA: And how do you prepare yourself for this grand effort? You get drunk, you roam the streets, you brawl, you pick up strangers, you make yourself sick…all this saddens my master.

BACON: Let's say it's just apprentice behaviour, shall we?

PAREJA: Look at these… (*Leafing through a sheaf of sketches.*) Mr Pamphili smiling, Mr Pamphili laughing, Mr Pamphili down in the mouth. Mr Pamphili pensive… Why not try Mr Pamphili with no expression at all?

BACON: He's not an easy subject. And he won't keep still.

PAREJA: After your last failure to make something out of him, my master Don Diego Velazquez said to me: 'Luis, it takes a slave to understand a slave. If he asks for the model again, you deal with him. Bacon fills me with too much pity and shame.'

BACON: Oh, we can't have that, can we?

PAREJA: He also suggested I should tell you no responsible craftsman works when he's been drinking. If he does, and something good comes of it, the credit goes to alcohol.

BACON: I'll remember that.

PAREJA: He recommends self-denial.

BACON: That is my wish also. May I get started?

PAREJA: I haven't said yes yet. You'll have to do something for me in return.

BACON: What?

PAREJA: A small thing.

BACON: Tell me!

PAREJA: Teach me how to paint like you.

BACON: The slave of Velazquez is asking me for painting lessons?

PAREJA: I'm already too like him. I've copied him until I'm doubly his slave. And Don Diego is so conscious of his own status, so bound up with himself, so serious about his own career, he couldn't teach anyone anything. But you're different. You like young people.

BACON: I'm no good at teaching. I'm much too soft. Can't criticise the young at all. They seem to have everything worth having.

PAREJA: Everything you paint is a criticism.

BACON: Are you any good?

PAREJA: When my master is out of the studio I find a scrap of canvas and bring out a few worn-out brushes he thinks I've thrown away, and I paint in secret.

BACON: All you need to do is carry on. Just keep on painting and let things happen.

PAREJA: King Philip came to the studio to see my master's recent work. I had to put all the new canvases up against the wall for him to look at. I included one of my own.

BACON: The more I hear, the more I think I can't teach you anything.

PAREJA: The King did not single it out as inferior in any way. I had painted it exactly in my master's style, but a bit better. Afterwards, I told the King what I had done.

He went back and examined the picture closely and said: 'Any man who has this skill cannot be a slave.'

BACON: There you are. Now, may we get on?

PAREJA: You don't understand. I want to paint like you, not him. I want to paint freely, what I see, what I feel. Teach me. I'll work hard. First of all I'll clear this place up.

BACON: You will not!

PAREJA: It's filthy, covered in dust.

BACON: I use the dust.

PAREJA: What for?

BACON: I put it in with the colours.

PAREJA: See, you've taught me something already! *Arriba! Arriba!*

POPE INNOCENT X, dressed as he is in the Velazquez 1650 portrait, enters.

PAREJA clears things out of his way.

BACON smiles with delight and relief, taking INNOCENT's arm to conduct him to the throne.

BACON, Oh, my dear Mr Pamphili. How good to see you. You look absolutely lovely, as always. Let's hope I can do you justice this time.

INNOCENT: Huh.

INNOCENT sits on the throne.

BACON: I don't know what I'd have done if you hadn't turned up tonight. It could have been the end, my deah. The absolute end.

PAREJA adjusts INNOCENT's robes and the positioning of his arms and angle of his head, putting him in the exact pose of the Velazquez portrait.

BACON whispers in INNOCENT's ear.

Papa, darling, you're not really looking grouchy enough.

INNOCENT frowns.

That's better. (*He steps back and looks at the composition.*) Now, there's something missing. Where's your bit of paper? You should have a paper in your left hand. Ah, perfect. (*Pick up a brown envelope out of the mess.*) Here, you can hold my income-tax demand.

BACON puts the envelope in INNOCENT's left hand, adjusts the angle of it, then steps back again.

Let's just check the original, shall we?

BACON picks up an art book from the mess and opens it at a well-thumbed page. They look at it together, glancing frequently at INNOCENT.

Near enough, wouldn't you say? (*He gives the book to PAREJA.*) Mr Pamphili, you're looking very sexy, my deah.

INNOCENT: Get on with your work. And don't breathe over me.

BACON: When I've finished will they say – this great pope was lucky to be captured and executed by Bacon?

INNOCENT: Spare me your childishness.

BACON starts to sketch.

PAREJA collects dust and puts it in a mortar with colour powders and grinds with a pestle.

BACON: Papa, the second finger of your left hand isn't in the right place. (*To PAREJA.*) Sort him out for me, will you?

PAREJA repositions the finger.

INNOCENT: Again, I suppose, you will deliberately paint my picture so it offends?

BACON: I'll paint it for you to hate, dear.

INNOCENT: Why do you waste your time and mine this way?

BACON: Assisi when you know how.

INNOCENT laughs.

BACON slaps him.

Keep still!

INNOCENT: That hurt.

BACON: Good.

PAREJA: Does hitting him help?

BACON: Of course, my deah. This Pope's to be thrashed into a quaking jelly. There's not an organ that can be left in a state of rest. All his defences must crumble. He has to be torn apart so we can see what's inside.

PAREJA: This is the second thing I've learnt from you.

BACON: Don't take any shit from whatever it is you're painting. A cardinal rule, eh, Papa?

PAREJA laughs.

Pause.

For a moment it seems BACON might hit him.

PAREJA: Aren't you glad if we laugh at your jokes? I'll try not to in future.

BACON: It's a long time since I've heard anyone laughing in this room but myself. Come here, youth.

PAREJA goes to him.

BACON kisses him on the cheek.

Another tip. Always look at what's underneath.

BACON takes INNOCENT's hat off.

INNOCENT covers his head.

You see how it changes him? How much older he looks. (*To INNOCENT.*) Have we caught a glimpse of the bald patch, then? And what have you got hidden under that marquee incarnadine? A nappy because you're incontinent these days? A veritable vineyard of varicose veins, my deah? And on a bad day your arsehole must look like a crown of bleeding thorns.

PAREJA: My God!

BACON: Always plumb the depths. That's where the flashiest diamonds lie.

INNOCENT: (*Pause.*) Francis, my son, what is it you want of me?

BACON: (*Tearing up the sketch he's been doing.*) Every time I look at what Velazquez put into your old carcase, I think – why did the Spaniard give him so much?

INNOCENT: Perhaps he only gave me what I already had?

BACON: Tell me something: when you saw the finished painting, did you like it?

INNOCENT: It has great power.

BACON: Yes, it certainly has that.

INNOCENT: Francis, I have studied theology – all the great heresies and errors – but you remain a mystery to me. You're wrong about everything, but so wrong I can't put my finger on the source of your confusion.

BACON: Best not to try.

BACON returns the hat.

INNOCENT: Thank you.

BACON: Put it back on.

INNOCENT: The slave will do that.

BACON: Can't you put your own hat on any more?

PAREJA: I must obey His Holiness.

INNOCENT: Come over here.

PAREJA goes to the throne.

Stand behind me.

PAREJA obeys.

(*Handing him the hat.*) Crown me.

PAREJA holds the hat over INNOCENT's head. He starts to lower it.

Wait!

PAREJA halts the descent of the hat.

We're making a moment here, Francis. What do you
see? A space between the top of my head and my hat.
It is the space Velazquez filled with splendour and
understanding.

BACON: (*Who has resumed sketching.*) I might have got
something here.

*PAREJA, still holding the hat out, walks round and looks
over his shoulder.*

PAREJA: A circle?

BACON: Not bad for a hand-drawn effort.

PAREJA: But a circle is only a circle.

BACON: Could you do any better? I've been up all night
but look at that. Not a tremble.

INNOCENT: Did you understand what I was saying?

BACON: Every word. And you're right. A pope is paid to
be right. (*To PAREJA.*) It's more of an ellipse, really. An
egg-shaped hole. (*To INNOCENT.*) Any kind of meaning
upsets me, really. When anything's finished there's
nothing left, is there? Are you with me?

INNOCENT: No.

PAREJA: What is the egg for?

BACON: His mouth. I build from the mouth outwards. The
mouth is the beginning.

INNOCENT: (*Placatory.*) Francis...

BACON: You spoke?

INNOCENT: Perhaps I was harsh.

BACON: If a model talks too much, my advice is – put something in its mouth.

PAREJA: Why is the mouth so important?

BACON: Ask him. The word was made flesh, wasn't it, Papa? And it was eaten. Everything passes through the mouth.

PAREJA: Holy Father, may I put your hat back on? My arms are getting tired.

INNOCENT: What's going to become of you, Francis?

BACON: I've no idea.

INNOCENT: Nothing is going to come of this picture. You're wasting your time. You don't understand me, or my function, at all.

BACON: I need the money. I've invested a lot of time and energy into it already. And I need the money.

INNOCENT: Why not offer your services to your new queen? Paint her portrait instead of mine. That might get you noticed.

BACON: I prefer old queens like you. They always have more to offer.

INNOCENT: (*Beckoning PAREJA to put the hat on him.*) You're a fool to yourself. You'll never get me right. You refuse to understand the necessities.

BACON: I can't stand people who think they mean a lot.

INNOCENT: Then why don't you leave me alone? I have to mean a lot.

BACON: Papa, you've got away with too much for too long. And too much has gone on lately.

INNOCENT: You give yourself no chance to succeed; and I'm sure that, somewhere, given you make the right choices, the talent could flourish, Francis. But my hopes for you are fading.

BACON: (*To PAREJA.*) I hope you're listening. This is how great patrons – and great models – have always influenced the living arts. He nags, I soak it up. Eventually, I'll do as he wants and glorify him. Isn't that right, Mr Pamphili?

INNOCENT: You deliberately choose not to follow what I'm saying.

BACON shows INNOCENT the second sketch.

(*Recoiling.*) Horrible!

BACON: (*Tearing it up.*) Not horrible enough for me, I'm afraid. You'll have to look much worse than that.

INNOCENT: Can't you at least show some respect!

BACON: Is that what you want, Papa? Respect?

INNOCENT: So do you. Otherwise, why would you paint?

BACON: (*Drawing again.*) You can't eat respect, you can't drink it, you can't fuck it, so who needs it? Stand up, deah.

INNOCENT: Why?

BACON: I want to use the commode.

INNOCENT: Use the one in the bathroom.

BACON: It's too far to go. Come on, move yourself.

INNOCENT gets off the throne.

BACON lifts the lid and has a piss.

INNOCENT: You do this every time.

BACON: (*To PAREJA.*) Tell him.

PAREJA: It's nothing personal, Your Holiness. He needs to humiliate his subject before he can paint it.

INNOCENT: That much I already know, you idiot! What I don't understand is WHY!

BACON finishes pissing and puts down the lid of the commode. Pause. He suddenly sits on the throne.

BACON: Oh, I'm suddenly rather tired. Don't get enough sleep in this business. (*Pause. He feels his injured mouth.*) You so remind me of someone.

INNOCENT: I do?

BACON: Someone on his way out of my life…out of everyone's life…out of life itself…someone who doesn't mean anything to me any more, but did…someone who wants to give me a past that was never there. I don't want a past. I don't want a present. And a future…well, if the past has no meaning it can't repeat itself.

INNOCENT: (*Gently.*) Francis, why haven't you told me this before? Now I can understand.

BACON: Told you what? I've told you nothing. I make it up as I go along.

INNOCENT: (*To PAREJA.*) Luis, go to the kitchen and make some coffee. I want to talk to Francis in private.

PAREJA exits R to the kitchen.

Pause.

INNOCENT bridles, using a different body language

(*In an East End accent.*) Well, now your wog pal has gone we can talk. Where did you pick him up?

BACON watches INNOCENT closely.

That's my chair, isn't it?

BACON: (*Getting up.*) What did you say?

INNOCENT: You heard.

INNOCENT swaggers over to the throne and sits down.

I leave you alone for five fucking minutes and you're off whoring. I don't want you dirty. I don't want you contaminated. That's an insult to our relationship, which I thought was a real one. And you said you loved me. Maybe it was in the heat of the moment, but you did say it.

BACON: (*Shouting.*) Help!

PAREJA runs on.

Hold my hand!

PAREJA: (*Taking his hand.*) What happened?

BACON: He came. He came.

PAREJA: Who came?

BACON: A visit.

PAREJA: Did you see anyone, Your Holiness?

INNOCENT: He's gone now.

PAREJA: But there was someone.

INNOCENT: As far as I could see.

BACON: Now I can make a start.

PAREJA: (*To BACON.*) What must I learn from this?

BACON: Never paint alone. By the way, Mr Pamphili – did you pay Velazquez or did Velazquez pay you?

INNOCENT: The honour of painting my portrait was enough.

BACON: Did Velazquez say this before he started work or after – before he knew you, or when he was recovering from the experience?

PAREJA: He was doubtful at first. The portraits my master had done of King Philip of Spain were worrying in their unwavering truthfulness and accuracy.

BACON: Not your line at all, eh, Mr Pamphili?

INNOCENT: I agreed to be painted, didn't I? Doesn't that speak for itself?

PAREJA: But he did give my master a gold chain and a medallion.

BACON: Bribed with a gold chain. I could do with one of those.

INNOCENT: See, you aspire. You're the same as everyone else.

BACON: Worse, my deah. Much worse. I'd like to be tied from head to foot in gold chains.

INNOCENT: And your affectation is to pretend to be a great sinner when you're only a little boy who's never grown up.

BACON: Not at all. I'm absolutely sincere about sinning and I was grown up from birth.

INNOCENT: Bless you, Francis. Don't despair. We'll find a way.

BACON: Bless me all you like, but nevah, nevah forgive me, Pope darling. That would be the absolute end. I'd be ashamed to feel shame.

Clock chimes three.

PAREJA: You must stop work, Francis, and let His Holiness do his office.

PAREJA takes a small book from his doublet and kneels in front of INNOCENT, holding it up for him to read.

INNOCENT puts on a pair of spectacles and leans forward, peering at the page, lips moving.

BACON works on a large drawing.

(*To BACON.*) The Pope is working. At three o'clock in the morning Pope Innocent says Vigils and Lauds of the Dead...

BACON: (*Muttering as he works.*) Oh, never forget the dead, my deah!

PAREJA: ...and Nocturns for All Saints. The Pope was trained to do this. The bell rings, he salivates verbally.

INNOCENT: (*His rapid mumble becoming audible.*) *Munda cor meum ac labia mea, omnipotens Deus, qui labia Isaie prophetae calculo mundasti ignito.* (*Subsides into unintelligible stream of Latin.*)

BACON: How many of these chats with the dead did you have while Velazquez painted your portrait? And could he keep pace with you, office for office? Six o'clock and Matins for you, get up with a hangover for me.

PAREJA: He says his Misere Anthems of the Cross and the BVM, you're already slapping it on.

BACON: I paint until my hangover goes away, which it does with surprising speed once I get into my stride.

PAREJA: At six forty-five he moves onto Prime and seven penitential psalms and you pause for coffee. At eight o'clock he says Terce and another five psalms for the dead.

BACON: Oh, the dead, the dead. While he's doing that I have a good shit, a shower and a shave, then get back to work. While he says Sext and sings mass at noon, I put down my brush, change into some glad rags, then rush down to the club where I get pissed as quickly as possible and start being brilliant at the bar.

PAREJA: Your average working day is over. Except for the crucial blood and champagne shifts, of which this is one.

INNOCENT: (*His mumbling becomes intelligible.*) *Dominus sit in corde meo et in labiis meis, ut digne et competenter annuntiem. Evangelium suum.*

PAREJA: At four-fifteen His Holiness is doing Vespers. You begin to seek your Evening Star. Compline at six for Papa, and you find your nocturn company, a star cold, remote, beauteous and beastly, tough, strong, having no pity. He'll make you quake, he'll make you cry.

PAREJA closes the book.

Synchronous blackout.

In blackout, the BBC Home Service early morning weather forecast for June 2nd, 1953.

As lights fade up, BACON is working.

INNOCENT sits on the throne.

PAREJA is offstage, in the kitchen he can be heard singing happily to himself.

BACON: It's going to piss down for the coronation. They're all going to get very wet. I expect the sun shone down on yours as it does upon the righteous.

INNOCENT: I don't remember.

BACON: Sure to have done. How long did your sessions with Velazquez generally last?

INNOCENT: Short stints. Unlike you, he was thoughtful, considerate, respectful – a complete gentleman

BACON: Oh, deah! What can I say? You don't like me. And I thought we were getting on so well together.

INNOCENT: And his conversation was wise, intelligent and delightful. The time just flew by.

BACON: Oh, don't get the wrong idea. I can be charming.

INNOCENT: You surprise me.

BACON: I'm quite nice, really.

INNOCENT: It wouldn't occur to you that I might appreciate some of that charm?

BACON: You wouldn't know what to do with it, my deah.

INNOCENT: I could try.

BACON: I'm very particular where and how I employ my charm. It only gets used on the rougher end of the market.

INNOCENT: Why is that?

BACON: So they can abuse and desecrate it, as it deserves. Try a grim little smile.

INNOCENT: Do you want teeth?

BACON: Ugh!

INNOCENT: My tongue? (*Sticks it out.*)

BACON: No, thanks.

INNOCENT: Think of the Word.

BACON: What's in that letter?

INNOCENT: (*Looking at it.*) It's a demand for fourteen pounds ten and eightpence.

BACON: No, no. Between ourselves, you and me, what's in that letter?

INNOCENT: Oh, I don't know. A scrap of paper you make me hold.

BACON: Yes, I make you hold. So, I have some power over you, don't I? And you've never bothered to even glance at it until I told you to. It might have had something to do with my soul, my spirit…but you wouldn't have been interested, would you? Look at it again.

INNOCENT: I don't want to.

BACON: Now it says: This picture was made by Velazquez, Anno Domini 1650, then ruinously superseded by Francis Bacon, Anno Domini 1953. Thanks be to God and the delicate bristles of the hog.

INNOCENT smiles.

Hold that.

INNOCENT: Hold what?

BACON: You smiled just like HIM. I'll start again.

Tears up the work he's done.

PAREJA enters from the kitchen with a pot of coffee.

BACON: Ah, at last. Won't be long. I need a shit.

INNOCENT: (*Clutching the arms of the throne.*) You're not coming on here. There is a limit.

BACON: Oh, no there isn't. (*Exits L.*)

Pause.

INNOCENT and PAREJA watch him go then look at each other.

PAREJA puts the pot of coffee down on the floor and squats beside it.

Pause.

INNOCENT: What do you think?

PAREJA: Difficult.

INNOCENT: Less for you than for me.

PAREJA: He makes fun, but he knows what he's doing. He's out to destroy you, then recreate you, Papa.

INNOCENT: A futile quest by a soul in a state of tormented flux. I've done enough. We should withdraw.

PAREJA: The penance is only complete when he's finished the picture.

INNOCENT: Then we must help him find what he's looking for! I can't sit on my hands must longer. I sometimes feel urges rising up, voices in my head telling me to rid the world of such a killer.

PAREJA: He will explain. He wants to. In fact, I think it's all he wants.

INNOCENT: It's a terrible penance I've been given, Luis. I only wish I hadn't deserved it. (*Pause.*) He likes you.

Lavatory is flushed off. Shower is heard working.

PAREJA: Yes.

INNOCENT: I hope he finishes before I explode. Oh, what a punishment he is!

BACON: (*Shouting from off.*) You can pour that coffee now, in theah! Won't be long.

PAREJA: He needs you the same way he needs his pain.

PAREJA gets up, then pours the coffee.

INNOCENT: Oh, I know, I know. I should be more charitable.

PAREJA: My master Velazquez painted the truth about you. This man wants to change it.

INNOCENT: But why? Why?

PAREJA: Things have got worse. The truth has become offensive. The hope is blighted.

INNOCENT: What sin we're dealing with!

PAREJA: But whose, your Holiness?

BACON enters with the clothes he was wearing in a bundle under one arm, drying his hair with a teatowel with the other hand, and wearing a towel round his waist. He throws the clothes down beside the throne and takes the cup of coffee from PAREJA.

BACON: Thank you, Luis.

PAREJA: You live in such confusion.

BACON: You know why.

PAREJA: Fungus is growing in the cupboard.

BACON: Take the lid off a tea-pot. Inside is a brew three years old with tiny spots of brilliant jade floating on it. In five years, who knows what I'll find? An undiscovered colour, perhaps?

PAREJA: A new colour? Could there be such a thing?

BACON: You were fortunate to live in a time when it was thought possible.

INNOCENT leans forward, peering, then snatches the towel away.

INNOCENT: (*East End accent.*) Let's have a look, here. Christ, Francis, someone's given you a good going-over, haven't they?

BACON: Give me that!

BACON grabs the towel and puts it back on.

INNOCENT: You're black and blue.

BACON: A walking palette, you see, Luis? Do you ever look at your own body?

PAREJA: Of course.

BACON: With a little effort, every part of the spectrum can be found there. You should work on it.

INNOCENT: Who did that to you, Francis? Worked you over like that?

BACON: An artist, obviously.

INNOCENT: I'll kill him, whoever it was.

BACON: (*Moving away.*) Excuse me.

INNOCENT: Come on, be nice.

BACON: Why d'you have to hound me?

INNOCENT: I'll fix whoever did that to your face. I'll find him and pulp the bastard. No one does that to my Francis and gets away with it.

BACON: (*As he exits.*) Except you, of course.

INNOCENT: (*Calling after him.*) I'll get him! When I've finished his own mother won't know him.

Door slams.

Pause.

PAREJA and INNOCENT look at each other.

PAREJA: Now the questions are: will he come back? And will you let Papa come back?

INNOCENT: (*East End.*) I'm not moving. I'm staying here.

PAREJA: I don't think Francis will come back until he knows you've gone.

INNOCENT: Wanna bet? He needs me. He puts me into everything.

PAREJA: To get rid of you.

INNOCENT: Nah!

PAREJA: I'll bet you a gold chain he doesn't want you any more. I think he's seen a way to do his picture without you being here.

INNOCENT: How?

PAREJA: He's going to kill you.

INNOCENT: You're on. (*Calling.*) Can't live without me. Can you, Francis?

PAREJA: You came too often. The living should not be a nuisance to the dead.

INNOCENT: I come when I like.

PAREJA: You've made your final entrance, I think.

BACON re-enters briskly and picks up a sketch pad and charcoal stick.

INNOCENT: (*To PAREJA.*) Told you.

BACON: If you're determined to hang around, do keep quiet and sit still.

INNOCENT: (*To PAREJA.*) That's a gold chain you owe me, sunshine. (*To BACON.*) Why did you sneak off from the club, like that? One minute we were having a nice drink and a chat about the evils of Cubism – I turn my back for a minute and you've sneaked off.

BACON: I was bored.

INNOCENT: Well, I was bored too, as it happens. But I wasn't fucking rude about it, was I? You went off looking for trade, didn't you? Some fucking squaddy on leave. I've told you before, Francis: you can get hurt that way.

BACON: He wasn't a squaddy at all. Actually, he's a captain in the Queen of Tonga's entourage. He's riding in her coach at the coronation.

INNOCENT: Christ almighty, Francis. You want to watch out. He could be a fucking cannibal.

BACON: All the better. But, if you must know, he's quite a sophisticate. His grandfather played canasta with Robert Louis Stevenson.

INNOCENT: When I catch up with him he'll wish he'd never been born. I'll mangle him. I'll cut him to ribbons. I'll throw his bollocks to the dogs. Who does he think he is, knocking great artists around? He might have broken your painting finger.

BACON sets up an easel and canvas with PAREJA's help, its back to the audience, as INNOCENT speaks.

Anyhow, I don't believe what you've said. You're protecting someone. I know what a tart you are. I know what's been going on. You don't care who you go with. Anyone'll do. Any rubbish. Come on, tell me. I'll forgive you.

BACON: I don't want your forgiveness.

INNOCENT: Hey, steady on, Francis…

BACON: I don't need you. You're dead.

Pause. BACON looks at his sketch, then at INNOCENT and back again, comparing them. He hands the sketch to PAREJA.

Hold this for me.

He starts to transfer the work on the sketch to the canvas.

INNOCENT moves restlessly.

INNOCENT: Was he big, this Tongan?

BACON: Enormous.

INNOCENT: Black?

BACON: All over.

INNOCENT: Are you going to see him again?

BACON: I'm meeting him later. He's going to be in his uniform. Then I'm going to ride in the carriage with him at the coronation. God knows what I'm going to wear, my deah.

INNOCENT: (*Relaxing, relieved.*) Got it. You're joking. For a moment you had me fooled.

BACON: I'm not fooling. You're dead.

INNOCENT: Don't say that, please, Francis, even for a joke.

BACON: The blow has been struck. From behind. Show some surprise. (*Shows him a rough sketch of the screaming Pope.*) Like that.

INNOCENT: That's supposed to be me? I don't believe it!

BACON: You talk too much. You always talked too much. You're one of those people who can't bear to be silent, to listen, to wait until you've got something interesting to say. You just have to open your big mouth and release the sewage in your mind. It's very annoying, especially at parties.

INNOCENT: What's this for, this picture?

BACON: I've got to get some money together.

INNOCENT: I'll scare you up some money. How much d'you need?

BACON: Couple of hundred.

INNOCENT: Two hundred? That's easy. I can get it for you by the end of the day. Make it two-fifty.

BACON: I'd rather you didn't. What I get for this I can quadruple at the casino.

INNOCENT: I've seen you lose.

BACON: Nevah a loser! Nevah!

INNOCENT: Good old Francis. That's my boy. Anyone interested?

BACON: Sainsbury might be, at a pinch.

INNOCENT: Why would he want a dead pope?

BACON: Cold meat at a bargain price.

They laugh.

INNOCENT: That's more like it. That's more like the Francis I know. You need your friends, you know, your real friends. I don't want anything. I'm not like the others, always after you to give them pictures so they can sell them when you're famous. I'd never do that. Not my style.

BACON: What's this about style? Your trouble is you haven't got any, my deah.

INNOCENT: (*Pause.*) Francis. I know what's happening. I know what people are saying to you about me. I'm nothing but a millstone round your neck, an embarrassment. You don't think of me like that, do you?

BACON: Do shut up, will you?

INNOCENT: I only asked.

BACON: (*Angrily.*) You take up too much room in my life! Go on, get out of here! Get thee to a graveyard!

BACON rushes over and grabs INNOCENT, pulling him out of the throne.

INNOCENT: (*Dropping the East End accent.*) *Per signum Crucis de inimicas nostris libere me!*

BACON: (*Letting him go.*) That's better, that's better.

INNOCENT: How dare you molest me!

BACON: Molest? No, Your Holiness. Adjust. The folds of your skirt had got out of line, my deah.

BACON goes back to work.

PAREJA looks over his shoulder.

PAREJA: I think I've worked out your technique.

BACON: That's more than I have.

A clock strikes.

PAREJA looks enquiringly at INNOCENT.

INNOCENT nods almost imperceptibly.

PAREJA slips off R.

BACON: (*Unaware of PAREJA's exit because he is focused on his work.*) Want to talk, Papa?

INNOCENT: As you wish.

BACON: I regret the second world war had to end.

INNOCENT: Really? How original of you.

BACON: All that desire in the streets.

INNOCENT: For a man to wish war not to end could be the worst of all sins.

BACON: London only came alive when it was being bombed. It was a happy, happy time for everyone. Since the victory everything has gone terribly downhill.

INNOCENT: God forgive you.

BACON: I paint so he won't.

PAREJA: (*Off.*) *Arriba! Arriba!*

VELAZQUEZ enters with FLAMINIA, another painter at the court of Innocent the Tenth in 1650, to whom he is giving drawing lessons.

PAREJA follows them in.

VELAZQUEZ and FLAMINIA bow and curtsy to INNOCENT.

VELAZQUEZ then takes BACON's sketch pad out of out of his hands, tears the top sheet off, crumples it up and throws it away, then gives the pad to FLAMINIA with a charcoal stick taken from behind BACON's ear.

FLAMINIA starts to draw INNOCENT.

VELAZQUEZ points to what FLAMINIA has done so far.

VELAZQUEZ: Why did you start with the nose?

FLAMINIA: To me, a nose is a beginning.

VELAZQUEZ: Isn't that strange? I would never think of doing that.

INNOCENT: Being in the hands of a master is very restful, eh, Flaminia?

VELAZQUEZ: If the Holy Father died before you got any further, which God forbid, all you'd be left with is… (*Kisses the end of her nose.*)

FLAMINIA: The beginning. The best time for all things, Diego.

VELAZQUEZ: Oh, God. Don't say that. If that's the case ours is almost over.

INNOCENT: I've been looking forward to this sitting all day.

VELAZQUEZ: Would Your Holiness condescend to look at the start Donna Flaminia has made? It would give her great encouragement.

INNOCENT smiles and holds out his hands.

FLAMINIA gives him the sketch.

He looks at it.

INNOCENT: The word is deft.

He hands the sketch back to FLAMINIA.

While this is going on, BACON pads around the studio, muttering to himself, rubbing his head. Finally he sidles up to INNOCENT.

BACON: I lied to you earlier, darling. There was no Tongan, as you might have guessed.

INNOCENT: You have the wrong pope.

VELAZQUEZ: (*To FLAMINIA.*) Try another orifice. (*Kisses her.*) That one.

FLAMINIA: Let me borrow your eraser, master.

VELAZQUEZ laughs and holds up a finger.

FLAMINIA kisses it, then uses it to rub out part of her drawing. Then they passionately embrace.

BACON sniffs the air like a dog, scenting their excitement.

VELAZQUEZ and FLAMINIA sit and draw together, both hands on the charcoal, smiling.

PAREJA: (*To INNOCENT.*) My master originally came to Italy to buy paintings for the King of Spain's collection, as you know, Papa. The great wave of beautiful work continuously breaking over him – Titian, Tintoretto, Veronese – has flushed out his inner needs. These giants of paint had to be equalled in deeds of flesh at least or he would be crushed for ever. It was in this mood, with a new love, that he set out to paint you; and it is this same flesh that has brought him to a halt.

INNOCENT: We must be patient.

PAREJA: I have the temerity to mention this to Your Holiness because slaves see everything and must share.

VELAZQUEZ: I have taught you how to draw, Flaminia. Now you must teach me how to live.

FLAMINIA: I could draw before, and you have lived before.

VELAZQUEZ: No. Not like this. I have been in a cage.

FLAMINIA: But in your skill you seem to know all the secrets there are.

VELAZQUEZ: I seem to, but I don't.

FLAMINIA: I am with child.

Pause.

PAREJA: Fifty was a dangerous age for my master.

VELAZQUEZ: Let me see.

FLAMINIA gets up and stands side on.

FLAMINIA: It doesn't show very much as yet.

VELAZQUEZ: How long?

FLAMINIA: It began on the day you started work on the Pope.

VELAZQUEZ: Madonna expecting a child. That's one I hadn't got round to, so far.

FLAMINIA: Oh, don't paint me like this. Paint me when I'm slender again.

VELAZQUEZ: I must find a way to get going on the Pope.

FLAMINIA: You mustn't worry. When the child is born, I'll give it away.

VELAZQUEZ: My love, I don't like asking you this – but will you go now? When you're here I seem to have too much to think about.

FLAMINIA: Of course. I'll go and see if I can develop this nose into a complete personality.

FLAMINIA exits with a passing smile at INNOCENT.

He gives her a wave.

Pause.

INNOCENT sighs, shakes his head, stands up, puts his hands behind his back.

INNOCENT: This cannot go on. Unless some progress is made soon, the work will have to be abandoned.

VELAZQUEZ: If I had known I would fall so hopelessly in love…

INNOCENT: Why should I be a victim of your carnality?

VELAZQUEZ: I crave your understanding, Your Holiness. I didn't ask for this to happen. I will fight my way out of it somehow.

INNOCENT: (*Pause. He walks up and down, thinking. Then, to VELAZQUEZ.*) What is it you're looking for?

VELAZQUEZ: A moment.

INNOCENT: Which must be why I sit here for hours.

VELAZQUEZ: I will make all those hours into one moment.

INNOCENT: And will that moment be this one? That hasn't been the way of it so far. You seem to have let every moment go.

VELAZQUEZ: When the portrait is finished – as it will be when this love has passed – no one will be able to look at it in any time and say: this is what I see now.

INNOCENT: Why is that?

VELAZQUEZ: Because it will not be then, in their time, but in the time that I shall make for you, then you will make it for them.

INNOCENT: Then this moment you speak of does not exist until you paint it?

VELAZQUEZ: It cannot.

INNOCENT: Are you sure?

VELAZQUEZ: I am more certain of that than my salvation.

INNOCENT: You must excuse the sloppiness of this Pope on doctrinal matters, but I thought only God had the power to create time.

VELAZQUEZ: I submit that anyone can make time, Your Holiness.

INNOCENT: Ah, but that kind of time is made out of what time there is already.

VELAZQUEZ: Then it follows that time can be used twice.

INNOCENT yawns.

BACON: Hold that!

INNOCENT: Uh?

BACON: Yawn again. (*Yawns himself.*) That's it. Something infectious. Something wide open. Something cavernous. And your gorgeous fillings, my deah. What a gold mine. One yearns for a pair of pliers and a pawnbroker.

INNOCENT yawns again.

BACON yawns again.

VELAZQUEZ yawns.

INNOCENT: It's outrageous! You come here, exhausted by your fornications, and expect me to sit for you while you regain your strength! This goes on day after day after day! It never entered your head to conserve your energies for my picture? Leave her alone for a while. (*Pause.*) Be warned. I sit here for the last time. (*To BACON.*) You! Fool! While he paints, you earn your wages and amuse me.

INNOCENT sits on the throne and takes up the pose.

PAREJA adjusts the folds of INNOCENT's robes.

Come on! Hurry! (*Very angrily.*) Why should all Christendom wait on what's between every wo…

PAREJA: (*After a brief pause.*) There is one other thing we could try. Quite often in the past the condition has been eased by letting his cockatoo out of its cage to stretch its wings.

Pause.

BACON, VELAZQUEZ and PAREJA look at each other.

VELAZQUEZ: Well, I'm not going that far even for the Pope.

BACON: Part of a fool's job, would you say?

PAREJA: Do you want to do it, Francis?

BACON: Not particularly, but meat has never frightened me.

BACON crawls under INNOCENT's robes.

VELAZQUEZ: Have you no shame?

BACON: (*From under INNOCENT's robes.*) None at all, my deah!

Pause.

Well! What have we heah?

BACON shrieks with laughter and moves around under INNOCENT's robes.

VELAZQUEZ: Ugh! How can he?

PAREJA: He will do anything to get close to the subject. Beat it, eat it.

VELAZQUEZ: But this…so demeaning…so unclean and disgusting, even for a fool.

BACON: Stand by!

INNOCENT's jaws clack shut. He flaps his arms like wings.

INNOCENT: Who's a pretty boy, then?

BACON crawls out from under INNOCENT's robes.

BACON: Well, he's in full working order now, bless him. Let's not waste any more time. Back to work, Don Diego! Let's get this thing finished one way or the other!

BACON and VELAZQUEZ work side by side.

As they do so BACON copies VELAZQUEZ. He takes peeps at what VELAZQUEZ is doing, rushes back to his own canvas, pulls faces, chuckles, apes VELAZQUEZ' posture with the brush and palette.

INNOCENT: Is this all there is to your fooling? You're not cheering me up at all. Tell me a joke.

BACON: I nevah tell jokes, my deah, they're too structured, if you know what I mean. But I do tell pointless stories. Here's one. Have you ever been to Siguenza?

INNOCENT: Siguenza? Where is that?

VELAZQUEZ: In my country – two days ride northeast of Madrid.

BACON: There's a cathedral I went to, once. I can't remember its name...

VELAZQUEZ: Santa Maria la Mayor.

BACON: One isn't allowed to wander about. When the tour's finished visitors are herded into the vestry to buy postcards. Hung behind the door is the most amusing thing I've ever seen – Christ on the Cross wearing rather a fancy underskirt.

INNOCENT: No!

BACON: Just like yours, my deah.

INNOCENT: (*To VELAZQUEZ.*) Do you know the works of art in this cathedral?

VELAZQUEZ: There is an Annunciation by El Greco. Not one of his best, but good enough.

INNOCENT: Do you know anything about a Crucifixion in an underskirt?

VELAZQUEZ: No, your Holiness. Would you like me to make enquiries?

INNOCENT: Wouldn't you have heard of such a strange piece of work?

VELAZQUEZ: I have heard of a local tradition amongst the peasant artists of Siguenza whereby they insisted upon depicting Our Lord naked, in all his maleness. Later, loin-cloths were added for the sake of decency.

INNOCENT: But not underskirts?

VELAZQUEZ: Not to my knowledge.

INNOCENT: Of course, the fool could be lying.

BACON: The hem was lace, beautifully painted. It must have taken ages to do. I wondered what the artist must have been thinking.

INNOCENT: I will never go to Siguenza.

Enter OLYMPIA, the Pope's mistress, in identical robes to those worn by INNOCENT.

OLYMPIA: Still at it? Come on. Lunch is waiting at the club. If we don't hurry, the oysters will lose their tang, the champagne will freeze solid and burst the bottles.

INNOCENT: Is it that time already?

OLYMPIA: You can bring this lot in as guests if you like, but only as long as they're good. Oooh, my arse is numb with all that sitting. How are you getting on? (*Looks at what VELAZQUEZ has done.*) Not very far. And the fool is painting too, bless him. How sweet. By the way, darling – my artist asked if you could give him a teeny bit of time tomorrow to sit for the reverse of a medal he's making.

INNOCENT: The reverse of the medal?

OLYMPIA: Well, I'm on the front, naturally. And for some reason he wants to draw you sitting at a spinning-wheel.

INNOCENT: A spinning-wheel? What's he got in mind?

OLYMPIA: Difficult to guess what he's got in mind, or whether he's got any mind at all! He also said he'd like you in a wimple.

INNOCENT: A wimple? Never.

OLYMPIA: Well, to save time I've had to agree. The Council of Florence need this medal urgently. They want to hang it round the neck of some argumentative writer of theirs, then garrotte him with it.

OLYMPIA sits on INNOCENT's knee.

This is the one you should really paint. Scrap the portrait you're doing. Do us together like this, two happy popes.

VELAZQUEZ: May I have your permissions to withdraw? A sudden migraine… (*He stumbles off holding his head.*)

OLYMPIA: That's right, run away! Guts are the last thing we need!

INNOCENT: Well, that seems to be that for this morning. Will you get up, dear?

OLYMPIA: (*Getting off INNOCENT's knee.*) How will we ever get anywhere if he can't face up to things? (*To BACON.*) Hey, you! Fool!

BACON: Me?

OLYMPIA: Yes, you! How many fools are there around here?

BACON: How may I serve?

OLYMPIA: I see you've been playing the artist.

BACON: Only to amuse His Holiness.

OLYMPIA: Tell me, if you were a real painter, would there be anything you'd be afraid to paint?

BACON: Nothing.

OLYMPIA: Yes, I'd be afraid to paint nothing. (*To INNOCENT.*) Darling, if I were you I'd swap Velazquez for this fellow. You might find yourself getting somewhere. Don't be long. (*Exits.*)

Pause.

BACON looks at INNOCENT, smiles, shrugs, looks at his canvas.

INNOCENT: The truth is, she's always been an embarrassment to me, but I can't possibly live without her.

BACON: Oh, I don't know. You might be able to.

INNOCENT: So you see, from within my own life I understand you Francis, but I cannot be seen to understand, you understand?

BACON: I understand.

INNOCENT: Because the Book of Leviticus forbids a man to uncover the nakedness of his brother's wife, every night, before I get into bed beside her, I have to forgive myself. That's hard.

Pause.

He lowers his head and sighs.

Francis, I am not fit for my great office.

BACON: Who is, deah?

INNOCENT: I feel it, you know.

BACON: Feel as much as you can, is my motto.

INNOCENT: Is it because of fascination with my sin that you need to paint me over and over again?

BACON: Oh, no. Nothing as easy as that. I did no research on you, Papa.

INNOCENT: Perhaps it was a protest against the papacy not opposing authoritarian regimes?

BACON: Good Lord, no. It is one.

Pause.

INNOCENT: Francis, son, how do we live with ourselves?

BACON: We work, Papa. (*Shows INNOCENT the canvas.*)

INNOCENT: Lord, save us! What an abomination!

BACON: You don't like it? (*Rips up the canvas.*) I don't like it either.

INNOCENT: Thank you, Francis. What a relief.

BACON: Now I'll have to start all over again with another mouth. (*Draws a circle.*) But the more I do you, the more meaning I wear away.

INNOCENT: What a sad case you are. Francis, don't you realise, the more you paint me, the more powerful I become?

A clock strikes twelve.

PAREJA enters dressed as an altar boy, carrying a tray with a silver chalice and salver covered with a white lace cloth.

For the sake of your soul, will you receive the body and blood of Our Lord at my hands?

BACON: I have no soul and I'm not hungry. You carry on.

INNOCENT: If you will not take it from me, then I will take it from you.

BACON: I don't give comfort to anyone.

INNOCENT: From such hands as yours I can receive redemption of a sort.

BACON: Not from me, Papa.

INNOCENT: I need forgiveness from somewhere.

BACON: And you think you're powerful?

INNOCENT comes down and kneels beside PAREJA, facing BACON. He reaches up and uncovers the chalice and salver.

INNOCENT: You don't have to believe in it. Just do it for me.

BACON: I think I've got all I want. (*Steps back and looks at the canvas.*) I'm finishing early today. Going to wash my hands and get down to the club.

BACON puts his brushes on the salver, then wipes his hands on the white cloth.

PAREJA bends down to whisper to INNOCENT.

INNOCENT whispers back.

PAREJA: (*To BACON.*) Are you saying that His Holiness is released?

BACON: Yes. He can go. I won't be needing him again.

INNOCENT: But you haven't made any progress!

PAREJA: And I've still got a lot to learn!

BACON: Well, my deahs, it's been an enormous pleasure but I really must get on.

INNOCENT: Have one more try.

BACON: Papa, I only ever wanted to get you wrong.

PAREJA: Through you I was going to get my freedom.

BACON: Not from me, youth.

BACON picks up the Velazquez art book and rips the relevant page out.

INNOCENT gets to his feet in fury.

INNOCENT: You even destroy your own inspiration! I hope there's a special circle of Hell for people like you!

BACON: If there is, it's probably called Soho.

INNOCENT: You have to finish the picture for my sake! It's my penance, my pain. If you don't succeed I will never be forgiven.

BACON: Don't worry, Papa. You're finished. In here. (*Taps his head.*) Goodbye. I hope we never meet again.

INNOCENT: I pray to God you're telling the truth. (*Pause.*) Now, I have my office to say. I doesn't matter where I am, it must be done.

BACON: Then I'll leave you to it.

A telephone starts to ring.

BACON rushes around the studio trying to find it.

Don't just stand there, help me!

INNOCENT looks for the telephone.

The ringing gets louder and louder.

BACON gets more and more frantic, throwing things aside.

PAREJA watches him, letting him get wilder and wilder, then goes to the throne, lifts the lid of the commode and brings out a telephone.

PAREJA: It's for you.

BACON runs over and snatches the phone from PAREJA's hand and claps it straight to his ear and mouth.

BACON: Darling, thank God you didn't ring off…oh, don't bother to apologise about last night. It was nothing. A silly tiff. No, I wasn't really hurt at all…all right, if you prefer it then, I was hurt! Is that better?…oh, your poor hand…

INNOCENT: (*Over BACON's telephone conversation.*) May God have mercy upon you, and forgive you all your sins, and bring you to life everlasting. Our affair is over.

While BACON is talking on the phone INNOCENT prays.

BACON: But of course I want to see you again...no, no, you won't have any trouble with him... Got him out of my system completely at last. It really is all over, thank God...well, he's got no choice but to accept it, has he?... No, don't come round here... I want to go out. I've been stuck in here all morning... I'll sign you in at the club. There're lots of people I want you to meet... Of course they'll like you, why shouldn't they?... I said NO, not here, this is my work-place... I don't want you here! Look, I'll give you the address of the club. Get a taxi... Where are you?... Where? (*He leaves the phone and looks out of a window, then returns.*) It doesn't matter. I don't care. I won't let you in!

BACON replaces the telephone and closes the commode.

He sits on the throne.

Long pause.

BACON watches PAREJA receiving the host from INNOCENT.

He goes off R.

A door catch is set.

A loud knocking at the door.

It's open!

BACON runs off to the door.

STRANGER: (*Off.*) Hello, Francis.

The door is heard closing.

BACON: (*Off.*) I told you not to come round.

The sound of a slap, off.

STRANGER: (*Off.*) Don't piss me around, Francis.

BACON: (*Off.*) I don't want you here.

Another slap, off.

(*Shrieking, off.*) You bastard! You bully!

STRANGER: (*Off.*) How d'you live in such a fucking mess? We'll have to get you sorted out, won't we?

The STRANGER beats BACON up, off.

BACON: (*Off.*) Harder! Harder!

STRANGER: (*Off.*) You're nothing, fucking nothing!

BACON: (*Off.*) Make me bleed!

INNOCENT and PAREJA exit sorrowfully towards the fracas.

Allegri's 'Miserere' over BACON's rising cries of pain.

Blackout.

End of Act One.

Act Two

Lights up on the Colony Room club bar and four very high stools reached by ladders. BACON as Pope Innocent is perched on a stool at the bar with VELAZQUEZ, OLYMPIA (now in court dress) and FLAMINIA.

BACON: My deahs, I'm not saying I'm right about everything but I do know a thing or two about art.

VELAZQUEZ: Your Holiness has impeccable taste.

BACON: Of course, Diego, darling – otherwise I'd never have asked you to paint me, would I?

They all laugh gently.

FLAMINIA: (*To VELAZQUEZ.*) Maestro, has any sitter ever had the gall to hate the portrait?

VELAZQUEZ: Not since I was taken under King Philip's wing.

They laugh again.

BACON: And now, with my blessing on your brushes, you can't go wrong, can you?

They laugh again.

OLYMPIA: There's a storeroom somewhere in the Vatican where all the unhung pictures of the Popes are kept, but I've never been able to find it.

FLAMINIA: Why would you want to?

OLYMPIA: To see where I'll end up.

They laugh again.

BACON: Covered in dust!

They laugh again.

I feel an encyclical coming on.

VELAZQUEZ, FLAMINIA and OLYMPIA lean attentively towards him.

Pain shares four letters with paint.

They applaud lightly, swaying on the stools.

Meaningless suffering minus pity plus ecstasy equals life's truth.

They applaud lightly again.

OLYMPIA: Don't be taken in. The cunt never means a word she says.

BACON: Nevah, my deahs, nevah!

They laugh again.

(*Shouting.*) Let's have some drinks heah!

VELAZQUEZ: Share more of your wisdom with us, Holy Father.

BACON: Ah, I approve of eagerness in the ignorant. The second encyclical is on its way.

VELAZQUEZ: Before that comes, Your Holiness, perhaps you would further explain the first? I'm still struggling to understand…

BACON: Try and keep up, Diego, darling. You're much too slow. Stand by. Here it cometh! Number the twain! The nature of art is that it hath no nature.

OLYMPIA: Fuck me! Bang on, eh? That was worth waiting for.

BACON: It only hath a presence, a presence ruined by any attempt at character or story.

OLYMPIA: What an illuminating cunt you are. If they'd heard it, that one would have all your critics queuing up to kiss your arse.

BACON: Ah, if only, my deah. But you'd never allow them into the club, would you? (*Shouts.*) Let's have some service heah! Where's the barman? Drinks all round and fresh horses for the men immediately, deah! (*Pause.*) To develop my theme: there is only the life-impact, which is the nail, and the hammah of meat knocking it home. Discuss.

FLAMINIA: Would you say all that again?

BACON: Certainly not. I never repeat what I say in case I catch myself out.

PAREJA enters with four goblets and a jug of wine on a tray.

About time too! Where've you been? Come on, pour, pour. We're all dying of thirst, heah! (*To FLAMINIA.*) So, what's your opinion since you can't be bothered to understand mine?

FLAMINIA: Surely, Holy Father, if there is a human figure in a painting a character or story is implicit.

BACON: Really? You amaze me.

FLAMINIA: A landscape without a figure is meaningless.

BACON: Then only landscapes are true. The third encyclical.

FLAMINIA: Why would anyone want to look at meaninglessness, let alone pay for it?

BACON: Nearly a relevant remark, deah. Where you go wrong is in the assumption that a figure, even a human figure, will retain its humanity in art. It doesn't. It becomes something else.

Pause. They lean forward.

FLAMINIA: What?

BACON: You agree, don't you, Diego?

PAREJA is listening as he pours the wine.

VELAZQUEZ: This is beyond me, Your Holiness.

BACON: (*To PAREJA.*) We'll look after ourselves now, but keep it coming, my son.

PAREJA exits.

Light purging darkness around the meat, my deahs. That's all art is about.

FLAMINIA: Not much of a philosophy.

BACON: Could Plato paint? The human story, so-called, only disguises the emptiness upon which pure light playeth so painfully.

OLYMPIA: Take no notice. He's only trying to start an argument with herself.

BACON: When it cometh to reality, only the Pope / Is able to cope. What number encyclical was that?

OLYMPIA: We've lost count, you pompous cunt.

VELAZQUEZ: (*Starting to get down from his stool.*) If Your Holiness will excuse me. An attack of vertigo.

BACON: Stay where you are! What's the matter with you? Can't you drink like a man?

VELAZQUEZ: I feel dizzy.

BACON: Too many oysters for lunch. If you sit there long enough and hold them down, you'll be all right. And there'll be a bonus for you, Flaminia. He'll get a hard-on you could chain a heretic to.

OLYMPIA: Come on, Diego. If you're a guest at my club, you have to be cheerful.

FLAMINIA: He's exhausted, poor lamb. He's put more into this portrait than anything else in his whole career.

VELAZQUEZ slumps forward, his head in his arms on the bar.

BACON: Oh, don't take on so.

VELAZQUEZ: (*Raising his head.*) Your Holiness has been very patient with me. Due to my own lack of self-control the portrait took up far too much of your valuable time. I am ill with guilt over that. While I floundered, Christ's work was neglected. The Church faltered. That thought is difficult for a religious man to live with.

FLAMINIA: (*Comforting him.*) But there's only the mouth left to finish, isn't there?

BACON: Hasn't he got that right, yet?

VELAZQUEZ: Hundreds of times I've tried but it never looks as it should.

FLAMINIA: We wondered if Your Holiness would allow me to do the mouth and finish the portrait since it's proving to be such a problem for Diego.

BACON: What? A woman give me a mouth? Nevah!

FLAMINIA: I have an idea how it should look.

BACON: If he cannot complete the picture then either leave it as it is, or have the thing destroyed as an abortion. Art is about delivery in full. If it doesn't work, burn the thing! Burn it! Another encyclical, nay, a bull! Ho, there! More drinks! (*To FLAMINIA again.*) And a word of advice to you, my deah. As an artist yourself you should never help the competition. If they're worth anything, they'll always help themselves.

PAREJA enters with more wine.

PAREJA: Any thoughts about my freedom yet, master?

VELAZQUEZ: Don't bother me now.

PAREJA: Even though a slave must always obey, and can be told to do anything, including unnatural and cruel acts, I never thought I'd descend to the level of being a jumped-up club bartender living off tips. Set me free, master.

VELAZQUEZ: This isn't the time.

PAREJA: I could finish the portrait better than she could. I've watched every brush-stroke you've made for thirty years.

BACON: I'd never agree to being painted by an artist who is a slave.

PAREJA: But a slave can paint!

BACON: Maybe, but he can't be an artist, eh, Diego?

VELAZQUEZ: He's been with me since the early days. In a way, I love the fellow. In fact, I've a suspicion he can paint rather well.

BACON: Then you certainly shouldn't give him his liberty. He may be better than you.

BACON roars with laughter.

VELAZQUEZ lowers his head and sobs.

OLYMPIA: I'm not having this. Who let that *conio lachrymoso* in here? Is he a member?

BACON: He's all member at the moment, deah.

FLAMINIA: Diego feels you have lost all respect for him.

BACON: An artist who depends upon the respect of anyone other than himself should give up and do something else. Nth sodding great incontrovertible encyclical of the day! Whoopee!

OLYMPIA: Charge your glasses! Papa's on top form! Wipe ten thousand ducats off his bar bill!

BACON: Thank you, deah. Now, what are we going to with this Hispaniardo? I've got no mouth, he's got no balls. Where do we go from here?

FLAMINIA: You've said too much. His heart is broken.

OLYMPIA: Well, it's liven up or he's out on his ear.

PAREJA: Your Holiness, there is an applicant for the post of papal fool outside. He's come round to the club to try and get an interview

BACON: Does he look a likely prospect?

PAREJA: He has a line of patter.

BACON: Let's see this fellow.

PAREJA exits.

OLYMPIA: Anything rather than listening to this doomstruck arsehole sobbing his heart out. He's really lowering the tone here. I can't run a club properly and keep the atmosphere genial with cunts like him around. Besides, he's getting me down. Can't you do something with him, Flaminia? Suck his cock for five minutes. That seems to keep them quiet.

VELAZQUEZ: My life is over!

BACON: Oh, Gawd. Here we go again. Angst and ye shall receive.

PAREJA enters, bringing INNOCENT, who now wears a black leather jacket and clothes the same as BACON's in Act One.

PAREJA: The applicant for the post of fool, Your Holiness.

INNOCENT bows.

OLYMPIA: He's too tall, isn't he?

BACON: And old, my deah. I'm not sure that I want an old fool. Well, I don't give you much of a chance, but let's talk. Can you tumble?

INNOCENT: I can tumble Your Holiness.

BACON: Good. Tumbling's essential round here. Tell me about yourself. Where were you born, and brought up, my good man?

INNOCENT: In Irish cracking country. I could ride before I could walk. My first fall was to the whips of my father's grooms. Tiring of this I became an itinerant comedian doing the clubs and castles. I've been here before but you were all too drunk to remember.

BACON: What a hard time you've had of it. And your method for making people laugh?

INNOCENT: First thing in the morning I work on the jokes I'm going to tell during the day. That keeps my hangover at arm's-length. Then there's a moment I treasure about seven-thirty when the nausea is transfigured into a sense of creative well-being. From that point on, I forge ahead. This takes me to lunch-time and my first drink.

BACON: Hilarious. And you carry on like this day in day out?

INNOCENT: Yes, Your Holiness. *Sans cesse*, as they say.

BACON: Amazing! What a constitution you must have.

INNOCENT: Would Your Holiness like to hear a joke I came by this morning?

BACON: Would I? Go ahead, my deah. This old codger is very promising, don't you think?

OLYMPIA: If he can keep it up.

INNOCENT: I can keep it up for months on end.

BACON: First class. What's your name, my deah?

INNOCENT: Francisco Pancetta, Your Holiness.

BACON: Well, Francisco, I'll toss you a challenge. (*Points at VELAZQUEZ.*) My guest, this Spanish gentleman, is in very low spirits. You know the kind of thing: despair with life, being in love, failure, all that malarky. If you can make him laugh the job is yours.

INNOCENT: Isn't that Signore Velazquez, the famous painter?

BACON: The same.

INNOCENT: Isn't he doing your picture?

BACON: Amongst other things.

INNOCENT: It would be an honour to help such a great man.

OLYMPIA: Never mind the bullshit. Get on with what you came for.

INNOCENT: There's a turn I do about a man who believes in nothing but meat.

BACON: Sounds just the ticket.

INNOCENT: May I have a moment to prepare?

BACON: Whatever you need.

INNOCENT bows and exits.

(*To OLYMPIA.*) What d'you think?

OLYMPIA: He's not really small enough.

BACON: Oh, he will be inside, my deah.

INNOCENT re-enters as a butcher.

What have we heah? Observe, Don Diego! I like the look of this.

OLYMPIA grabs VELAZQUEZ by the hair and lifts his head up.

OLYMPIA: This is all for your benefit, you snivelling tosspot, so keep your eyes open.

PAREJA enters, grinding colours in a mortar. INNOCENT brushes dust up from the floor and puts it into the mortar then spits into it.

BACON: (*Laughing.*) Excellent! So economical!

VELAZQUEZ groans.

PAREJA daubs INNOCENT with blood-coloured paint.

BACON shrieks with laughter.

INNOCENT: Is Signore Velazquez laughing yet?

BACON: No, but I'm sure he will. Keep trying!

INNOCENT: May I claim the right of the fool to mock his master beyond all limits?

BACON: Fire away!

INNOCENT: You won't lose your temper when I insult you?

BACON: Nevah!

INNOCENT: I might call you pretentious, cocky little fucker with a pea-sized brain.

BACON: Sheer bliss, dear boy.

INNOCENT: Holy Father, you're a man who's always taking the piss, right?

BACON: Right! That's my job!

INNOCENT: You find homo fucking sapiens very funny, dontcha?

BACON: Hilarious!

INNOCENT: The way we struggle and suffer brings joy to your deformed heart, don't it?

BACON: It do.

INNOCENT: This is what makes you tick, you evil fucker. Cut your throat and do us all a favour, will ya! Oh, I'm getting really worked up about how cruel and negative you are, Papa. I'm steaming mad with you!

BACON: Go on! Go on!

INNOCENT: I'm a butcher, perhaps, but at least I'm alive in my soul. You're a walking corpse, cold and heartless. I hate art. I hate you... I really do...you've got no right... Fucking painters! Who needs them?

BACON: Who indeed?

INNOCENT: Any sign of a change in Don Diego, Your Holiness?

OLYMPIA: Who cares about him? We're having a great time!

FLAMINIA: Holy Father, I beg of you, make him stop. Diego can't stand it.

OLYMPIA: Oh, tell him to go fuck himself. If he had any sense he'd be laughing his head off

BACON: What else have you got for us? I hope that's not all.

INNOCENT: Oh, no, Your Holiness. I've hardly got going yet.

VELAZQUEZ: This is a deliberate insult to my craft!

BACON: It isn't aimed at you, is it?

INNOCENT: Unthinkable that I should offer such a great artist any insult whatsoever, Your Holiness. It is merely an act.

BACON: I think you're doing very well. Don't be put off.

VELAZQUEZ: No more, I beg you…no more. Any painter who has spent as many years as I have perfecting his work, who knows the skill and care that must go into… (*Breaks down.*)

INNOCENT looks at BACON, silently asking for his permission to carry on.

BACON raises his goblet, smiling.

BACON: Carry on crucifying.

INNOCENT: I don't want to deprive the gentleman of his *raison d'être.*

BACON: My lad, do continue with the entertainment. The self, my self, any self, is there to be mocked, saith the Lord, then shattered and the pieces scattered like confetti in the universe. I'm convinced the point will come when Don Diego will just have to laugh at how funny that all is.

BACON climbs down off the throne, goblet in hand, to stand by INNOCENT's side.

What's next, fool? What's next? Keep it going!

INNOCENT: Has Signore Velazquez got a sense of humour at all?

BACON: Deep down, I'm sure he has.

INNOCENT: He's not showing it!

BACON: Keep digging, my deah!

INNOCENT: Don't worry, I haven't finished with you yet.

BACON: Oh, good.

INNOCENT: I hate you. You've made my life an instrument of torture. If you become successful as an artist it will mean the extinction of beauty. All artists will belong to an accursed race shunned by the rest of mankind.

VELAZQUEZ falls off his stool, moaning with horror.

FLAMINIA: His mind has snapped! Oh, what a deed has been done here today! His faith in art has been utterly destroyed. Why did you let the fool go so far?

BACON: My deah, you have just encouraged the emergence of a four-wheeler encyclical: when any limit is reached, it's time to rest it. (*To INNOCENT.*) That was most stimulating and invigorating. Take a breather.

INNOCENT: I'm afraid that's all there is, Your Holiness.

BACON: Nonsense. You're not trying. Ah, you're keeping the best part up your sleeve. Come on, let's have it. Diego is on the brink of giving in I'm sure. Then the post of papal fool is yours.

VELAZQUEZ lurches to his feet, rushes over and attacks INNOCENT with FLAMINIA hanging on to stop him.

VELAZQUEZ: Hateful iconoclast! What have you left us? A desert to live in! A wilderness, without hope, without redemption!

INNOCENT: I was only earning my living.

FLAMINIA: Holy Father, you have let this ape traduce and scorn everything we hold precious right under your nose. Why dismantle Diego's world? Torment his soul? You, who should be defending what is good and beautiful, have struck a terrible blow against truth!

BACON: Really?

FLAMINIA: Will it ever recover? Will it ever find shape and meaning again?

BACON: I hope not. (*To INNOCENT.*) A thousand thanks, fool. You've made my day. Now, if you'll give us a moment to see these two off the premises. We can continue. (*To FLAMINIA.*) Take the Spaniard away. We won't sit for him again. The portrait is cancelled. He can go back to Madrid as soon as he likes.

INNOCENT: No, I beg of you! Give me another chance. I couldn't meet the challenge. I failed to make him laugh. Without this job I'll starve.

VELAZQUEZ straightens up.

VELAZQUEZ: Please, do not be hasty, Your Holiness.

FLAMINIA: (*Aghast.*) You're not going to plead!?

VELAZQUEZ: Do you want this poor fellow to starve?

FLAMINIA: Oh, God! You're going to knuckle under! Is there anything sacred?

BACON: You are too proud for my taste, Don Diego.

VELAZQUEZ: I was not proud for myself...

FLAMINIA: I can't bear it! Everything you've ever believed in ruins and you can't stand up and fight! I despair of you! I'm going to get an abortion! (*Runs off, weeping.*)

VELAZQUEZ: She will come to understand. As I was saying, Your Holiness, I was not proud for myself but for my profession.

BACON: Fuck your profession. What you paint never makes me laugh in the right way.

VELAZQUEZ: What way is that, Father?

BACON: So it hurts.

INNOCENT: If Your Holiness will allow me... (*To VELAZQUEZ.*) I am your servant, sir. Please understand that sometimes a man is driven to make an impression beyond what he feels as himself. He strikes against the darkness. If I have in any way offended you, forgive me. I should add that being a fool – even a fool who is too tall to be a fool – implies a lack of perspective. I do not see clearly... I'm clumsy...hardly conscious of what I am destroying.

BACON: There we are. What could be more generous?

BACON goes back to the bar.

Have a chat with him, Olympia. He needs the warm words of a woman who's seen it all.

BACON helps OLYMPIA down off her stool.

She takes VELAZQUEZ aside.

OLYMPIA: The fool seems genuinely contrite. Give him another chance. Come on, laugh for him. Just a little one. He's been working hard. He deserves the job.

BACON: The smallest titter will suffice, Diego.

INNOCENT: (*Kneeling.*) Please, laugh and forgive. Your blessing, master.

VELAZQUEZ looks at him uncertainly, then at BACON who has an eye on him as he drinks at the bar.

VELAZQUEZ: (*Pitched so BACON can hear.*) How will it all end?

OLYMPIA: It's already ended. Give him a laugh and your blessing! What will it cost you?

VELAZQUEZ: (*With a tremor of disgust.*) I give you my blessing.

INNOCENT: Thank you, Don Diego, thank you. And forgiveness?

VELAZQUEZ: Oh, all right.

BACON: Next time you pick up your brush, Don Diego, remember how the fool found me: I am the enemy of self. I am the enemy of meaning. My left eye is atomic bomb. My right eye is smoke. I am oven-ready. I am meat. I am burning fat. I am blood. I am sperm. I am pain. I am instinct. I am womanless. I am childless. I am pitiless. I am the word. I am the flesh betrayed. Truth I am not. I mean not. I weep not. I do not open the book. I fall. I am infallible. I am the law. I am the unstoppable crime. I am the kiss of the cooling corpse. I am the burnt-off face. I am the cruel mirror. Back to front I hang crucified. I wear thorns. I dance on spears. I drink champagne vinegar. But I am not finished or forsaken. I cannot be caught. I am not who I am, or was, or will be. I am hiding in my mess. I am pottage. I am this inheritance. I am rare beauty about to go. I am strength turned inward. I am fearless. I am dying. I am going. I am gone.

VELAZQUEZ: (*Laughing.*) All that? And you're only the Pope!

BACON: (*To INNOCENT.*) He laughed.

OLYMPIA: About time.

BACON: I did the trick, but the job is yours.

Snap blackout.

Faint sounds of a street party outside and rain on studio roof window.

Lights up on BACON's flat and mess.

BACON stands staring up at the rain on the roof window.

PAREJA enters in a wet plastic mac and fifties clothes, with a shopping-bag of groceries.

PAREJA: You'll get a crick in your neck.

BACON: Actually, I'm trying to get rid of one.

PAREJA: Are we going to find somewhere to watch the procession go by?

BACON: I'm not.

PAREJA: We could watch on the pub's new television? They've got it rigged up in the bar.

BACON: You go if you like. I've got to work.

PAREJA: Come on, Francis. Take the day off.

BACON: I can't.

PAREJA: I like her.

BACON: Who?

PAREJA: The Queen. What harm does she do?

BACON: That's no reason to like anyone.

PAREJA: Want something to eat?

BACON: No, thanks.

PAREJA: That's a bit of a blow. I thought I'd do you a proper English cooked breakfast for Coronation Day.

BACON: I never eat breakfast.

PAREJA: What am I going to do with this lot? I only bought it for you.

BACON looks in the shopping-bag and takes out an egg, tossing it in his hand.

BACON: A beautiful thing is an egg. The old fresco artists used to put egg in their distemper to give it extra body. Would you like to do a fresco?

PAREJA: I'm not sure about frescos.

BACON: It's a picture painted on a wall.

PAREJA: Oh, yes. I've seen one somewhere.

BACON: The bathroom needs decorating.

PAREJA: Right!

BACON: You decide on the subject.

PAREJA: Can't think of anything.

BACON: Well, you're not much use, are you? The most famous of all frescos is by Leonardo da Vinci. It's of Christ's Last Supper. Ours could be Bacon's First Breakfast.

PAREJA: (*Laughs.*) Right!

PAREJA exits.

BACON sits for a moment in silence, listening to the sounds of PAREJA banging pans in the kitchen and the rain.

BACON: Come on. Come on.

INNOCENT enters in screaming pope mask and costume, propelling himself along in a wheelchair.

INNOCENT: Have you spoken irreverently of God, or holy things? Have you told untruths? Have you been zealous for God's honour, for justice and virtue? Have you faithfully resisted thoughts of infidelity, distrust, presumption, impurity? (*In an East End accent.*) Hello, Francis. Glad to find you at home. Still got my key. (*Shows BACON the key hanging round his neck on a gold chain.*)

BACON: You should have given it back when we… (*Tails off.*)

INNOCENT: When you gave me the boot? No one does that to me. I decide when I come and go.

BACON: Please leave me alone…

INNOCENT: I just came round to see how you were. Anything I can do for you?

BACON: I don't want you here any more.

INNOCENT: That's all right, then. I wouldn't want to stop you in the middle of working. Carry on. (*Sniffs.*) What's cooking? Or should I say: who's cooking? You don't hang about, do you? You finish with one and you start on another.

BACON: Don't spoil things for me.

INNOCENT: Why shouldn't I?

BACON: Please, be reasonable.

INNOCENT: I thought you liked me because I was unreasonable.

BACON: What can I give you that will make you go away?

INNOCENT: My place.

BACON: What place? This place? Have it! You're welcome. I'll move out.

INNOCENT parks the wheelchair exactly where the throne was in Act One.

INNOCENT: I'll never stop. I'll never leave you alone. I'll have your sanity off you, sunshine.

BACON: Why can't you know when these things are over?

INNOCENT: Why can't you know when they're not?

Pause.

He looks out of the window.

Everyone out there dancing in the pissing rain. It's the start of a new age, Francis. I used to think we'd go into it together.

BACON: (*Kneeling beside the wheelchair.*) Bless me, Father, for I have sinned.

INNOCENT: (*Dropping the East End accent.*) When was your last confession?

BACON: Nevah!

INNOCENT: This could take some time. Begin.

BACON: I don't know where to start.

INNOCENT: That is the root of your problem, my son. Let me help: Have you been obstinate in following your own will, or in defending your own opinion in things either indifferent, dangerous, or scandalous?

BACON: I have.

INNOCENT: How many times?

BACON: Ceaselessly.

INNOCENT: Have you taken pleasure in hearing yourself praised or yielded to thoughts of vanity?

BACON: I have.

INNOCENT: How many times?

BACON: Endlessly.

INNOCENT: Have you indulged yourself in overmuch ease, or in any way yielded to sensuality?

BACON: I have.

INNOCENT: How many times?

BACON: Overmuchly.

INNOCENT: Your penance is... (*In the East End accent.*) to throw him out and take me back!

BACON: Nevah!

INNOCENT: Then no *te absolvo* for you! (*Pause.*) Please, Francis...

BACON: No.

INNOCENT: I'm begging. (*Pause.*) We'll meet up now and then, won't we?

BACON: I never want to have to look at you again.

INNOCENT: Until I met you, I knew who I was. Now I don't recognise myself. You've altered me. I don't enjoy that feeling of not knowing whether I'm worth anything, Francis. How did you manage to do that to me? Before I met you people looked up to me. Maybe they were even a bit scared. Now I'm rubbish. What's the trick?

BACON: I want him. That's all the forgiveness I need.

PAREJA enters in a striped kitchen apron.

PAREJA: Do you want fried bread? (*Looks at INNOCENT in the wheelchair.*) Why are you always looking at that picture? I thought it was finished?

BACON: (*Sharply.*) Go back in the kitchen!

PAREJA: What's the matter?

BACON: Give me a moment, will you?

PAREJA: What are you so upset about?

INNOCENT: (*To PAREJA as he leaves.*) He'll scoop out your soul as if it were an oyster! He'll open up the world for you, then leave you nothing.

PAREJA: (*Looking at INNOCENT.*) I don't like it.

BACON: Did I ask for your opinion?

PAREJA: All right, all right.

PAREJA exits.

INNOCENT: He won't last long.

BACON: Oh, yes he will.

INNOCENT: He won't put up with it.

BACON: Wanting to learn helps…he's an outsider, an innocent.

INNOCENT: You may think you've finished with me, but you've not. It's not over. There's still work to be done. Right now you're thinking – thank God that's out of the way – a new start – but you'll need me again. I'm the one you'll always want, you'll always need. Once you've made him into a copy of me, and you've started cursing him for the world, and blaming him for your sins because he'll never have the power to forgive you, you'll prefer the original. I was strong when I came to you. I'm still strong. I'll stay strong, even though my heart is broken, which is why you've had to work so hard on me. But you'll break HIM, himself, the part we cling on to, which is the part of anyone you can't stand.

BACON: Absolutely, my deah!

INNOCENT: Why do you do it?

BACON: Because it's not meat.

OLYMPIA and FLAMINIA enter in fifties costume, very dressed up.

OLYMPIA: Hello, Francis. Get your coat. We've decided we're not allowing you to skulk here on your tod on Coronation Day. You're coming down the club to help us celebrate.

BACON: Terribly sorry, darling. I really am very busy…

OLYMPIA: I'm not taking no for an answer. (*Looks at INNOCENT.*) Who's this old cunt, then?

BACON: Oh, she was finished a while back. I've been waiting for the paint to dry, but the weather's been so damp it's taken ages.

FLAMINIA: Fuck me! It's devastating! Is it good?

BACON: Someone seems to think so.

OLYMPIA: Hurry up. Everyone's down there waiting. We can't start without you.

BACON: Since you put it like that, I suppose I'll have to give in.

FLAMINIA: (*Looking at INNOCENT.*) Has she just had a nasty shock of some kind?

BACON: (*Calling.*) Luis! Forget the breakfast, my deah!. (*Takes the handles of the wheelchair, starting to push INNOCENT off.*) Today we drink champagne in pints and it's all on me.

OLYMPIA: You're very generous all of a sudden.

BACON: He pays for everything. (*Exits, pushing INNOCENT.*) Someone's bought it!

FLAMINIA and OLYMPIA laugh and start to exit after BACON.

PAREJA comes out of the kitchen.

OLYMPIA looks him up and down.

OLYMPIA: Oh, you're new. Let's have a look. You'll do, but you'll have to be signed in. She's nice, isn't she?

FLAMINIA: Very nice.

OLYMPIA and FLAMINIA link arms with PAREJA and march him out, laughing.

The sounds of the street party get louder.

Then the rain comes down harder on the roof window. And drowns them out.

Snap blackout.

The End.